The Successful Immigrant Blueprint (SIB)

The Smart Way to Build, Thrive, and Succeed in a New Land

WRITTEN BY: SHOLA OYEWOLE

FIRST PUBLISHED IN 2025

SHOLA OYEWOLE

Foreword

- A message to every dreamer who left home for a better life
- Why this book matters now more than ever

Introduction: My Journey to the American Dream

- The first day: confusion, culture shock, and courage
- Lessons learned from early struggles
- What SIB is all about — a mindset, not a manual

Introduction 7

Chapter 1: 10

The Immigrant Advantage — Turning Struggle into Strength
.... 10

Chapter 2: 16

Leave the Victim Mentality Behind — Reprogramming Your
Mind for Success 16

Chapter 3: 23

Think Like a Boss, Not Just a Worker 23

Chapter 4: 31

Mastering the Art of Saving — The Immigrant's Quiet Power
Move 31

Chapter 5: 39

Smart Money, Smart Moves — Building Credit, Avoiding
Debt, and Keeping What You Earn 39

Chapter 6: 47

Building Your Own Table — Starting Small, Dreaming Big,
and Launching Your Business in a New Land 47

Chapter 7: 56

Ghost Mode — The Power of Focus, Silence, and
Consistency 56

Chapter 8: 63

Dare to Be Great — Breaking Fear, Thinking Bold, and
Owning Your Space 63

Chapter 9: 71

Financial Freedom — Mastering Money, Credit, and Discipline as an Immigrant 71

Chapter 10: 79

Building Your Business in a New Land — From Side Hustle to Structure 79

Chapter 11: 89

Networking and Building Community — The Power of Relationships in a New Country 89

Chapter 12: 99

The Emotional Journey — Handling Homesickness, Pressure, and Self-Doubt 99

Chapter 13: 108

The Immigrant Entrepreneur — Turning Hustle Into Legacy 108

Chapter 14: 117

Building a Legacy Beyond Borders — Giving Back, Investing, and Expanding Your Impact 117

Conclusion: 126

The 90-Day Action Plan: Turning Your Blueprint Into Results 131

-

SHOLA OYEWOLE

Introduction

Welcome to the Land of Possibilities

When you get off that plane, holding your bags and your dreams, the air smells different. You can almost feel the weight of hope pressing against your chest. You look around new faces, new systems, new rules and you whisper to yourself, *"This is it. My new beginning."*

But what nobody tells you is that **the dream isn't automatic**.
In America or anywhere you migrate to, your accent will be tested, your patience will be stretched, and your confidence will be questioned. You'll meet people who doubt you, systems that confuse you, and moments that will make you wonder if you made the right choice to leave home.

Yet, beneath all that uncertainty lies *the greatest opportunity of your life*.

The truth is that **immigrants are some of the strongest people on earth.** We start from scratch, build without a safety net, and find ways to win in systems we didn't grow up in. That's not weakness, that's genius wrapped in resilience.

Still, many immigrants get trapped in the same cycle:
Working long hours, chasing more shifts, sending money home, and posting online to "look successful."
They burn out, lose focus, and never step into the *freedom* they came for.

This book, *The Successful Immigrant Blueprint,* is your escape plan from that cycle.

It's not just about surviving; it's about *thriving*.
It's about learning how to think smart, save wisely, speak confidently, and build boldly.
It's about **becoming the boss of your own destiny**, not just another worker clocking in and out.

You'll learn how to:

- Master your mindset and drop the victim mentality.
- Save money and grow it — quietly.
- Polish your English and your confidence at the same time.
- Move in "ghost mode" — focused, silent, consistent.
- Build your own business, even while working a regular job.
- And most importantly, *dare to be great*, no matter where you start.

Because the truth is, nobody will hand you success, not in this country, not anywhere.
But if you're willing to grind with focus, live below your means, and think like a boss, **you can create the life you once dreamed of.**

I know, because I've lived it.
I've been the newcomer trying to find my footing. I've been the worker who stayed up late studying and saving. I've been the one who zoned out the noise and chose growth over validation. And if I can do it, so can you.

This is not a fairy tale. This is **a blueprint** — clear, practical, and real.

Follow it, and you'll not only survive in this country — you'll **succeed beyond imagination**.

So take a deep breath.
Forget what didn't work in the past.
Right now, this moment, is your restart button.

Let's begin your journey to becoming **a successful immigrant**, the kind who builds quietly, shines brightly, and inspires others to dream bigger.

Welcome to *SIB*.
Let's get to work.

Chapter 1:

The Immigrant Advantage — Turning Struggle into Strength

When you move to a new country, you don't just cross borders, you cross into a whole new version of yourself.

Every immigrant has a story. Some came here chasing education, others seeking safety, opportunity, or a better life for their families. But no matter how your story began, one truth binds us all - we *came here to win.*

And yet, the journey isn't easy.

You face cultural shocks, financial pressure, unfamiliar systems, and sometimes even silent rejection. You work twice as hard just to earn half the recognition. You juggle two worlds, the one you left behind and the one you're trying to build.

But here's the secret: **those same struggles that make life hard also make you unstoppable.**

That's the *Immigrant Advantage.*

1. Pressure Builds Diamonds

Every immigrant learns to stretch what they have — money, time, energy — and still find a way forward.
You become resourceful out of necessity. You figure things out when no one is there to explain.

That resourcefulness? That's your diamond.

When others quit, you adapt. When others complain, you create. You've been through enough uncertainty to know how to move in faith, not fear.

In a world full of comfort seekers, **your struggle is your strength.**

2. Hunger Creates Focus

Back home, you probably dreamed about "coming to America." But once you land, the dream flips; now you dream of *making it* in America.

That hunger to succeed, to prove yourself, to make your family proud, to show that your sacrifice was worth it — is what keeps you going.

Don't ever lose that fire.
Channel it. Direct it.
Let it fuel your education, your business, your personal growth.

The truth is *hunger beats talent when talent gets comfortable.*

So, while others are sleeping on their comfort, you're building your future one quiet grind at a time.

3. You Speak Two Languages — and That's Power

Many immigrants feel embarrassed about their accent or how they speak English. But let's be real, *speaking more than one language is not a weakness: it's a superpower.*

It means you can connect with more people, think in multiple ways, and adapt faster than most.
Don't hide your voice, strengthen it.
Your accent is not a barrier; it's your badge of courage.

You learned a new language in a new world, and you're still standing. That's power.

4. You Know How to Start from Scratch

You arrived here with little, maybe no credit, no network, no "connections." But what you *did* bring was grit, humility, and drive.

That ability to start over and still move forward. That's rare.
It's what entrepreneurs, leaders, and innovators are built from.

Most people fear starting over.
Immigrants live it and thrive anyway.

You don't fear humble beginnings because you've seen worse.
You don't wait for perfect conditions, you create them.

That's not weakness. That's *blueprint energy.*

5. Sacrifice Is in Your DNA

Let's be honest, we sacrifice more than most.
We work long hours.
We live below our means.
We send money home even when we're barely making enough.
We miss weddings, birthdays, and family moments just to build something better.

That level of sacrifice builds focus, discipline, and strength.

You've already done the hardest part — leaving home, starting over, and surviving.
Now it's time to build on that foundation.

You've proven you can sacrifice. Now, learn to *strategize* — to let your sacrifices multiply into something lasting.

6. You're Built for Adaptation

New country. New culture. New laws. New systems.
And yet, you adjust. You learn. You blend in just enough to move forward, while keeping your identity intact.

That's adaptability — a skill money can't buy.
And in a fast-changing world, adaptability is gold.

Immigrants don't just survive change — we master it.
That's why so many global CEOs, innovators, and entrepreneurs have immigrant roots. They learned how to turn uncertainty into strategy.

7. Your Struggles Are a Setup, Not a Setback

Every challenge you face, from rejection letters to language struggles to financial setbacks, is not proof that you're failing. It's proof that you're *building muscle.*

Pressure doesn't break people like us, it prepares us.

So don't curse your struggle. Study it.
Every experience is teaching you how to be sharper, wiser, and tougher for the success ahead.

Your pain has purpose if you pay attention.

8. Own Your Advantage

It's time to stop apologizing for being different.
You are not "less than" anyone.
You are *a walking story of courage, discipline, and survival.*

Own it. Speak proudly about where you came from.
Let your accent remind you that you had the courage to start over in a new world.

You didn't come here to blend in; you came to **build out**.
To write your own success story in a foreign land.

And the beautiful thing? You already have everything it takes.
You just need to think smarter, act bolder, and believe deeper.

Final Thought: From Survivor to Strategist

You've proven that you can survive. Now it's time to **strategize**. Stop living day to day. Start planning month to month, year to year.
Every paycheck, every class, every connection — make it count.

The Successful Immigrant Blueprint is not about luck.
It's about *discipline, mindset, and execution.*

Your story is not over.
You're just turning the page to the chapter called *"Greatness."*

Quote to End the Chapter:

"Immigrants don't wait for doors to open; we build our own and walk through boldly."

Chapter 2:

Leave the Victim Mentality Behind — Reprogramming Your Mind for Success

When Blessing first arrived in the U.S. from Nigeria, she was full of dreams. She had a master's degree, a solid résumé, and confidence that things would move fast. But three months later, reality had slapped her hard.

Her accent got mocked during a phone interview.
Her degree wasn't recognized by most employers.
She worked long shifts at a nursing home and came home exhausted, wondering if she had made a mistake, leaving everything behind.

One night, after another rejection email, she sat on the floor of her small apartment crying. "This country doesn't want me," she said to herself.

That's the moment it started — **the victim mindset**.

1. The Quiet Trap of the Victim Mindset

It often starts silently.
You work so hard, but things move slowly. You see others getting ahead. You feel unseen. So you start believing the system is against you.

You start saying things like:

- "If only I had American connections."
- "They just don't like immigrants."
- "No one wants to help me."

And slowly, that mindset becomes your identity.

It's not that you're lazy, you're tired. You've been fighting to belong, and no one seems to notice. But here's the truth that every successful immigrant eventually learns:
The system is tough — but your mindset can be tougher.

You can't control what others do, but you can control how you respond.

2. Everyone Starts Somewhere — Including You

I remember meeting a man named Carlos at a small entrepreneurship meetup in Boston. He came from El Salvador, and for years, he washed dishes in a restaurant. But every night after work, he would sit in his car with a notebook, writing down small business ideas.

"I didn't have a degree," he told me. "But I had eyes. I watched how people moved."

One day, when the restaurant's cleaning company failed to show up, Carlos offered to do it himself, for a small fee. He did such a good job that the manager told him, "If you start your own cleaning company, we'll hire you."

That was ten years ago.
Today, Carlos owns a cleaning business with twelve employees, and he's hiring new immigrants, giving them a start.

When I asked him what changed everything, he smiled and said:

"I stopped thinking the world owed me. I just started building quietly."

That's the mindset shift.
From *"Why me?"* to *"Watch me."*

3. Reprogramming How You Think

If you grew up in a culture where success is measured by titles or big houses, coming here can feel like a downgrade at first.

But survival isn't shameful.
Every doctor who drives Uber, every engineer working security, every cleaner paying tuition — *you are building your foundation.*

The key is not to stay stuck in "survival mode."

Here's how to reprogram your mind when you start feeling like a victim:

1. **Replace complaints with clarity.**
   Instead of "They don't hire people like me," ask "What skill do I need to make myself impossible to ignore?"

2. **Remember the long game.**
   Your first job is not your destiny, it's your training ground. Every experience adds value if you stay teachable.

3. **Talk to yourself differently.**
   Words have power. Replace *"I'm tired of starting over"* with *"I'm grateful I can start over."* Gratitude shifts your focus from what's missing to what's possible.

4. **Stop comparing your beginning to someone else's middle.**
Social media will lie to you. Everyone shows success, nobody posts their nights of doubt.

4. The Danger of the "Show-Off" Mentality

Many immigrants fall into another trap, trying to prove their success too early.
You buy the car, the designer shoes, the phone — not because you need it, but because you want to feel like you're "catching up."

But behind every show-off story is quiet anxiety.

I met a young man named Ade who worked two jobs. He always looked sharp, drove a new car, and posted "God did it!" every weekend. But when COVID hit and his hours were cut, he had nothing saved.

He told me later, "I was working to impress people who weren't even watching."

That's what the victim mindset does, it tricks you into performing success instead of building it.
Ghost mode — staying low and working smart- is how you break free.

5. Learn to Pivot, Not Pity Yourself

Every immigrant who succeeds learns how to pivot.

If your degree doesn't work here, go get certified.
If your accent gets in the way, take language classes or practice

with podcasts.
If your boss disrespects you, plan your exit strategy quietly.

Pivoting means adjusting your route, not quitting your journey.

I once met a woman named Rina from India who worked as a cashier for years, even though she was an accountant back home. Instead of giving up, she started volunteering to do small bookkeeping for her church. That volunteer work became her U.S. experience. Eventually, a member referred her for a job, and now she runs her own tax prep business.

Rina told me something powerful:

"I stopped saying 'I can't because I'm an immigrant.' I started saying, 'I can *because* I'm an immigrant. I know how to find another way.'"

That's the immigrant advantage in motion — resilience meets creativity.

6. Stop Waiting for Permission

Here's something most immigrants never hear:
Nobody is coming to rescue you.
Not your employer, not your school, not the government.

That's not bad news, it's freeing news.

Because once you accept that, you stop waiting for permission to move. You start doing. You start taking small steps — opening an LLC, saving aggressively, taking online classes, improving your English, or connecting with mentors.

Successful immigrants don't wait for the perfect time; they move while they learn.

7. From Victim to Visionary

When you stop thinking like a victim, your energy shifts.
You start seeing possibilities instead of barriers.

You no longer say, "They won't hire me."
You start saying, "I'll learn something that will make me unignorable."

You stop saying, "I'm just an immigrant."
You start saying, "I'm the reason my family will rise."

This shift doesn't happen overnight. It takes time, courage, and faith. But every small step toward confidence rewires your mindset from victim to visionary.

8. Your New Identity

From today on, you are not "a struggling immigrant."
You are a **strategic immigrant.**

You don't just work — you plan.
You don't just survive — you grow.
You don't just dream — you execute.

This new identity is what *The Successful Immigrant Blueprint* is all about: helping you build strength on purpose, not just by accident.

Final Thought:

There's no shame in starting small. The only shame is staying small because you kept making excuses.

So, stop blaming. Start building.
Stop performing. Start preparing.
Stop talking. Start executing.

Because no matter where you come from, **you belong in the room of success.**

◆ **Quote to End the Chapter:**

"You can't be a victim and a visionary at the same time. Choose one and build your story around it."

Chapter 3:

Think Like a Boss, Not Just a Worker

When Samuel first arrived in the U.S., he did what most new immigrants do: he looked for a job immediately. Within two weeks, he was working in a warehouse. The pay wasn't great, but it was something.

He worked hard, never missed a day, and even covered other people's shifts. But after three years, he realized something painful — nothing had really changed.

The rent kept rising, his savings never grew, and he was always too tired to think about anything beyond the next paycheck.

One day, while loading boxes, he overheard a conversation between his supervisor and a delivery driver. The driver owned his own truck and made twice what Samuel earned — working fewer hours.

That day, Samuel made a decision.
He said, *"I can't work like this forever. I need to think like a boss."*

1. The Worker Mindset vs. The Boss Mindset

Most immigrants are raised to believe that a good job equals success.
And in truth, there's pride in honest work, no shame in it at all.

But there's a difference between *working hard* and *working smart*.

The **worker mindset** says:

"Let me just make enough to survive."

The **boss mindset** says:

"Let me learn how money moves — so I can create something of my own."

Workers think in hours.
Bosses think in systems.

Workers wait to be told what to do.
Bosses find what needs to be done and build around it.

You can start with a job — that's normal.
But you shouldn't stay stuck in one forever if it's not leading you to growth.

2. The Hidden Trap of Comfort

The biggest threat to immigrant success isn't poverty — it's comfort.
Once you can pay your bills and send money home, you stop stretching.

That's where many people get stuck — in a loop of "okay."

You stop studying.
You stop networking.
You stop dreaming.

You start saying things like,

"At least I'm not suffering."
"This job is fine."
"One day, I'll start my own thing."

But *"one day"* never comes for most people, because comfort is the enemy of progress.

Thinking like a boss means asking yourself every few months:

- What's my next move?
- What skill can I learn next?
- How can I make my money multiply instead of disappear?

3. How Bosses Think Differently

Boss thinking isn't about ego — it's about vision.
It's how you approach life, money, and opportunity.

Here's how the shift looks:

Situation	Worker Thinking	Boss Thinking
Income	"I need a raise."	"I need another income stream."
Time	"I'm tired after work."	"How can I use my evenings to build something?"
Skills	"I do what they tell me."	"I learn what can set me free."

Situation	Worker Thinking	Boss Thinking
Problems	"It's not my job."	"Every problem is a potential business idea."

Bosses see opportunities where others see limits.

The man who starts cleaning offices after work might later own the cleaning company.
The woman who sells snacks at a hair salon might later open her own beauty line.
The worker who understands his company's system might later start consulting for others.

That's what happens when you stop seeing yourself as *just* a worker.

4. From Security Guard to Small Business Owner

I met a man named Hassan at a local immigrant networking event. He worked as a security guard for almost eight years. Night shifts, long hours, low pay.

But instead of complaining, Hassan used his downtime wisely. He started reading business books, watching YouTube videos on entrepreneurship, and writing down small business ideas in a notebook.

One night, he noticed how many small businesses in his city didn't have a website or online presence. He didn't know anything about web design — but he decided to learn.

Six months later, he built a simple website for a friend's barbershop for free. That project led to referrals. Soon, he started charging small fees. Within two years, Hassan quit his security job.

Now, he runs a small web design agency from his apartment.

When I asked what changed, he said:

"My mindset. I stopped thinking like a worker trying to survive and started thinking like a problem-solver trying to serve."

That's the boss mindset — not about being rich but being *responsible for your own path.*

5. Start Small, Think Big

You don't have to quit your job tomorrow.
You just have to start *thinking differently today.*

Maybe you start selling something small online.
Maybe you learn a digital skill in your free time.
Maybe you invest $100 monthly in a savings account or a small side project.

Small, consistent moves matter.

Every successful immigrant you admire today once worked long hours, but what made the difference was that they didn't stop there. They planned. They saved. They learned.

They built.

6. The Mindset of Ownership

Boss thinking is about **ownership**, not necessarily owning a business right away, but owning your decisions, your learning, and your progress.

You can be a boss even as an employee if you treat your job like your own company.

- Show up with pride.
- Learn the system.
- Build relationships.
- Ask questions.

That's how you gather experience to build your own thing later.

A true boss doesn't just think about money — they think about **impact**, **freedom**, and **legacy**.

7. The Fear Factor

Many immigrants never take the next step because of fear.
Fear of failure.
Fear of losing stability.
Fear of what people back home will say if things don't work out.

But what if you fail? You learn.
What if you lose? You adjust.
What if they talk? They will, whether you win or not.

Courage doesn't mean you're not scared; it means you move anyway.
That's how every business, every dream, every blueprint begins — with one brave step.

8. When You Think Like a Boss, Life Changes

You stop living paycheck to paycheck.
You stop chasing validation.
You start respecting your time, your effort, and your peace.

You start asking different questions:

- How can I make this $1,000 grow?
- What problem can I solve in my community?
- How can I create opportunities for others like me?

You begin to operate differently, with quiet confidence.
That's when you know your mindset has shifted.

9. The Blueprint Lesson

You came to this country not just to work, but to **build.**
You are more than your job title.
You are the CEO of your own life.

Every skill you gain, every dollar you save, every risk you take — it's part of your blueprint.

So, don't just chase a job.
Build a strategy.
Don't just work hard.
Work smart.
Don't just survive.
Own your story.

Final Thought:

There's nothing wrong with starting small, but there's everything wrong with staying small because you were afraid to think bigger.

Every immigrant who succeeded did one thing first — they stopped thinking like employees and started thinking like architects of their own destiny.

◆ **Quote to End the Chapter:**

"You can work for money or make money work for you — the difference starts in your mind."

Chapter 4:

Mastering the Art of Saving — The Immigrant's Quiet Power Move

When Tunde first got his job in the U.S., his first instinct was excitement. His first paycheck felt like gold — real dollars, clean cash, freedom in his hands.

He called his family back home to celebrate. "This country is sweet!" he said.

Within two months, he bought new clothes, upgraded his phone, and even started sending money home more than he could afford, just to "prove he was doing well."

But after six months, he realized something uncomfortable: he was working hard, but his bank balance was always close to zero. He wasn't poor, but he wasn't progressing either.

That's when he learned one of the most powerful truths in the immigrant journey:

Making money is not the same as keeping it.

1. Why Saving Is Power

In a world obsessed with showing off, saving is a silent rebellion.

It's saying, "I don't need to prove I'm doing well. I'm preparing to do better."

Many immigrants earn enough to build something great, but they spend like they're trying to impress people they left behind.

Saving money isn't about being stingy. It's about being *strategic*.

Because in a foreign land, money is your first form of security. It's what gives you choices, to go back to school, start a business, invest, or walk away from a toxic job without fear.

Saving gives you **freedom**, and freedom is wealth.

2. Story: The Woman Who Moved in Silence

There's a woman named Mary, originally from Ghana, who worked as a nursing aide for years. Her coworkers often laughed at her because she never went out or joined weekend shopping trips.

They called her "Miss Budget."

But what they didn't know was that Mary had a plan.

She saved quietly for six years, no designer clothes, no flashy car, no drama. Every month, she saved at least 25% of her paycheck.

Then one day, without warning, she resigned.

People thought she was moving back to Africa, until they saw her name on a new daycare business signboard.

Mary had saved enough to buy a small property and start her own daycare center. Within two years, she was employing some of the same coworkers who once mocked her.

That's the power of saving quietly — it makes noise later.

3. The Psychology Behind "Show-Off" Spending

Let's be honest, many immigrants feel pressure to *look successful.*
We want people back home to believe the dream is real. We want to show we made it.

So, we post, buy, display, and impress.

But the truth is, no one back home is paying your rent.
They'll clap for you online, but they won't send you $1 when you're broke.

You don't owe anyone proof of success.
You owe yourself **peace of mind** and **financial stability.**

That's what the wise call *"ghost mode."*
Work, save, and plan — quietly. Let your results speak for you later.

4. The "SIB" Saving Formula: Simple but Effective

You don't need complex math or a fancy finance degree.
You just need structure, discipline, and commitment.

Here's the **Successful Immigrant Blueprint Saving Plan (SIB Formula):**

Step 1: Pay Yourself First

Before rent, before groceries, before anything, save at least **15–25%** of your income automatically.
Set up a separate account if you have to. Make it hard to touch.

Step 2: Build an Emergency Fund

Life in a foreign land can be unpredictable.
Aim to save 3–6 months of your living expenses.
That fund becomes your safety net, your permission to take bold steps without fear.

Step 3: Cut Emotional Spending

Before every major purchase, ask:

"Do I need this, or am I just trying to feel good for now?"

Step 4: Separate "Home Money" from "Growth Money"

Supporting family back home is beautiful, but not at the cost of your own stability.
Always allocate a fixed, affordable amount for that. Don't let guilt drain your progress.

Step 5: Automate, Don't Debate

The less you think about saving, the more consistent you'll be.
Set automatic transfers to your savings or investment account.

Consistency beats intensity every time.

5. The Power of Living Below Your Means

This one truth separates the successful from the struggling:

The people who look rich too soon usually stay broke too long.

If your income increases and your lifestyle grows equally, you'll never get ahead.

Real growth happens when your income grows but your expenses don't.
That's how you build real wealth.

A new car might make you feel good, but it depreciates the moment you drive it off the lot.
A growing savings account, though? That buys you freedom, choices, and rest.

Living below your means isn't punishment — it's preparation.

6. The Couple Who Chose Peace Over Pressure

A Kenyan couple I once met, Mercy and Daniel, moved to the U.S. five years ago. They both worked full-time jobs but refused to live beyond their means.

While their friends rented luxury apartments, they lived in a modest one-bedroom unit.
They didn't eat out often. They used one car.

People said they were too "tight." But in four years, they bought their first home, cash for the down payment, no struggle.

Today, they own two rental properties and travel when they want.

Mercy said something that stuck with me:

"People were laughing when we were saving. But when we bought our house, the same people asked for advice."

That's how quiet consistency wins, slowly, then suddenly.

7. Your Money Reflects Your Mindset

If you can't manage $500, you won't magically manage $5,000. Saving is not just financial, it's emotional discipline.

It's saying, *"I choose my future over my feelings."*

When you start treating your money like a tool, not a toy, everything changes.
You become calmer, more focused, more strategic.

Because you're not chasing approval anymore, you're chasing purpose.

8. From Saver to Investor

Saving is the foundation, not the finish line.
Once you build stability, it's time to make your money work for you.

Learn the basics of:

- High-yield savings accounts
- Certificates of Deposit (CDs)
- Mutual funds or ETFs
- Real estate (even small, shared investments)

- Small business start-ups

    You don't have to invest big — you just have to *start small and smart.*

    That's how the quiet savers become the quiet millionaires.

9. The Blueprint Lesson

Every dollar you save is a vote for your future.
Every flashy purchase you skip is a step toward your peace.
Every quiet month you stay consistent moves you closer to freedom.

You don't have to announce your grind.
You just have to stay focused long enough to outlast those who waste their own potential.

Your wealth will speak one day, loudly and it will tell a story of discipline, not display.

Final Thought:

In the immigrant journey, saving money is more than financial advice, it's survival, strategy, and strength combined.

You came here to build, not to prove.
So save quietly. Build steadily.
And when it's time, let your results speak so loudly that you won't need to say a word.

- **Quote to End the Chapter:**

SHOLA OYEWOLE

"Don't spend to impress. Save to progress."

Chapter 5:

Smart Money, Smart Moves — Building Credit, Avoiding Debt, and Keeping What You Earn

When Ahmed first moved to the U.S., he was excited to finally receive his **first credit card.**

The email said, *"Congratulations! You've been approved for a $1,000 limit."*
To him, it felt like free money, so he spent it fast. A few online orders here, a new phone there.

He told himself, *"I'll pay it later."*

But later came with interest.
$1,000 became $1,300, then $1,500. Soon, the calls from the credit card company began.
His credit score dropped before he even knew what a credit score was.

It wasn't that Ahmed was irresponsible, he just didn't understand the system.
And that's the truth for most immigrants: **nobody teaches us how money really works here.**

1. Welcome to the American Credit Game

In America, credit is like oxygen, invisible but necessary.

You need it to:

- Rent an apartment
- Buy a car or house
- Start a business
- Even get some jobs

But here's the trap: the same system that can build you can also break you.

That's why financial success in this country isn't about how *much* you make — it's about how *smartly* you move.

2. The Smart Shift Worker

Let's talk about Lillian, a single mom from Kenya.
She worked long night shifts at a warehouse, always tired but determined.

One day, a coworker explained how credit worked: "It's not about how much you borrow, it's how responsibly you manage it."

Lillian listened. She applied for one low-limit credit card and made small, controlled purchases, gas, groceries, and paid them off early every month.

Within a year, her credit score went from *no record* to *excellent*.

That one move helped her get a car loan at a low interest rate. Two years later, she used her strong credit to buy her first home.

Same warehouse job.
Different mindset.

That's the **immigrant advantage**: we know how to maximize little things with patience and discipline.

3. Understanding Credit — In Simple Terms

Think of your **credit score** as your financial reputation.

It's a three-digit number (usually 300–850) that tells lenders if they can trust you with money.

Here's what affects it:

Factor	Description	Impact
Payment History (35%)	Do you pay bills on time?	Biggest factor
Credit Utilization (30%)	How much of your credit limit you use	Keep it below 30%
Credit Age (15%)	How long you've had credit	The older, the better
Credit Mix (10%)	Different types of credit (card, loan, etc.)	Shows maturity
Inquiries (10%)	How often you apply for credit	Too many can hurt you

4. The Blueprint for Good Credit

If you're new to the system, here's how to build a strong foundation:

Step 1: Start Small

Apply for a **secured credit card** or a **credit builder loan**.
Deposit a small amount ($200–$500), use it monthly, and pay it off early.

Step 2: Pay Early, Not Just On Time

Early payments build trust faster. Even paying a few days ahead helps your score rise steadily.

Step 3: Keep Utilization Low

If your card limit is $1,000, don't spend more than $300.
Credit is about discipline, not display.

Step 4: Check Your Credit Report Regularly

Use **Credit Karma**, **Experian**, or **AnnualCreditReport.com** (free) to track your progress.
Look for errors and dispute them if needed.

Step 5: Don't Chase Too Many Cards

Having 1–2 well-managed accounts is better than 6 cards you struggle to pay.

5. Avoiding the Debt Trap

Many immigrants fall into debt not because of greed, but because of misunderstanding.

We come from cultures where "credit" often means "trouble," so when we get access, we sometimes misuse it.

Here are a few smart truths to remember:

- **Credit is not cash.** It's a loan. Treat it like borrowed fire; it can warm or burn.
- **Pay more than the minimum.** The "minimum payment" is a trap that keeps you in endless interest cycles.
- **Avoid impulse loans or store cards.** Many retail cards have sky-high interest rates that eat your paycheck.
- **Debt equals stress.** Don't borrow peace away just to look comfortable.

6. The Couple Who Learned the Hard Way

Pedro and Lucia, from the Dominican Republic, worked two jobs each.
They earned decent money, but they were always behind on payments.

They financed new furniture, took out car loans, and maxed out store cards — all to "look like they were making it."

But debt doesn't care about appearances.

When their credit dropped, they couldn't qualify for a mortgage. That's when reality hit, they were working for the system, not for themselves.

So, they started cutting back: one card, strict budget, cash payments only for six months.

Slowly, their credit score rebounded.
Three years later, they finally bought their first home — *the right way.*

They said, *"We stopped impressing others and started building for ourselves."*

7. Smart Credit Habits That Change Everything

Here are a few practical daily habits that separate the successful from the stuck:

- **Automate your bills.** Never miss payments — it's the #1 credit killer.
- **Use credit cards for needs, not wants.**
- **Track your spending weekly.** Awareness is power.
- **Have one "growth card"** — **for controlled use and credit history.**
- **Avoid co-signing for anyone.** Protect your name.

  Remember, your **credit score is like your name in the financial world** guard it like your passport.

8. The Smart Immigrant's Money Triangle

To build long-term success, balance your money in three directions:

Direction	Purpose	Example
Savings	Security	Emergency fund, travel, goals
Investments	Growth	Stocks, business, real estate
Credit	Opportunity	Home loans, business funding

When these three work together, you stop being just a worker; you become a *strategic builder.*

9. Ghost Mode Money Discipline

The most powerful immigrants move in silence.

They don't tell everyone about their side hustles, their credit goals, or how much they save.
They focus, plan, and build quietly.

They understand this one rule:

"The quieter you move, the stronger your foundation."

When your money is right, your confidence changes. You walk differently, think differently, and attract better opportunities.

That's not luck, that's discipline rewarded.

10. Blueprint Summary — Smart Moves to Keep What You Earn

Build credit early, wisely, and slowly.
Use debt only for things that grow value, not to buy validation.
Keep utilization below 30%.

Pay early, track regularly.
Move quietly, plan boldly.

Final Lesson:

You didn't come all this way to be trapped by a system; you came to *learn it and win with it.*

America rewards the disciplined.
If you can master money, not just earn it, you'll always have power, no matter your accent, background, or origin.

Remember, the goal is not just to make money, but to **keep it, grow it, and control it.**

Quote to End the Chapter:

"Credit is not free money; it's borrowed trust. Use it wisely, and the system will work for you."

Chapter 6:

Building Your Own Table — Starting Small, Dreaming Big, and Launching Your Business in a New Land

When Ada first came to the U.S. from Nigeria, she dreamed of stability, a good job, a nice apartment, and some peace of mind.

She worked as a CNA (Certified Nursing Assistant), doing long shifts and saving bit by bit. But deep down, she wanted more than just to survive.

Her passion was cooking. Every weekend, she made jollof rice, puff-puff, and suya for her friends. They'd always say, "Ada, you should open a restaurant!"

At first, she laughed it off. "I'm just a small girl trying to pay rent," she'd say.

But one day, she realized — *every successful person once said those same words.*

So, she started small: meal prep orders from her apartment kitchen, posting pictures online, delivering food after her shifts.

Within a year, she had loyal customers. Within three, she opened **Ada's Kitchen**, a catering business that now employs three other immigrants.

She didn't wait for permission. She didn't wait for perfect timing. She just started — small, scared, but serious.

That's what this chapter is about: **building your own table instead of waiting for someone to offer you a seat.**

1. Why Every Immigrant Should Think Like an Entrepreneur

Many immigrants spend their best years chasing jobs, promotions, and titles — but the truth is, no job can give you full control of your destiny.

A business doesn't have to be big. It doesn't even have to replace your job immediately.
But it should be *yours*.

Something that grows with your effort, carries your name, and builds generational freedom.

Think about it:

- You left your home country.
- You adapted to a new system.
- You work twice as hard to prove yourself.

You already have the courage most people never find.
So why not use that courage to **create** instead of just **comply**?

2. From Uber Driver to Business Owner

Samuel, a Ghanaian immigrant, used to drive Uber full-time. Every day, he picked up tech workers who talked about startups and investments.

Instead of getting intimidated, he got curious.

He started learning, listening to business podcasts between rides, reading free resources online, watching YouTube tutorials about small business management.

One day, he noticed many of his riders were ordering food delivery late at night, but there weren't many local African food options in his city.

That was his light bulb moment.

He began a weekend side hustle, cooking and delivering Ghanaian meals on weekends.
He called it **AfroEats Express.**

Today, Samuel doesn't drive Uber anymore. His business delivers across three cities and has partnerships with catering events.

He didn't need millions — just **awareness, action, and consistency.**

3. The Power of Starting Small

Forget the idea that you need a huge investment to start. Most successful immigrant businesses started with little:

- A hairstylist renting a chair in someone's salon.
- A truck driver buying one truck, then two, then three.
- A cleaner turning weekend gigs into a registered LLC.
- A home baker selling cakes from her kitchen.

You don't need everything to start — you need to start with what you have.

The secret is **execution**.
You can plan forever, but until you act, it's just a dream on paper.

4. Blueprint Steps to Start Your Own Business

Here's a simple, realistic breakdown, designed for immigrants working full-time but ready to build something on the side.

Step 1: Identify Your Strength or Passion

What do people already come to you for?
Hair? Food? Organization? Driving? Babysitting? Graphic design?
That's your starting point.

Step 2: Start Lean

Don't rush into debt or expensive equipment.
Start with what's necessary, not what looks professional.
Growth will refine you later.

Step 3: Register Your Business

File an **LLC** (you can do it online in most U.S. states for less than $200).
That gives you credibility, protection, and access to business banking.

Step 4: Separate Personal and Business Money

Open a **business bank account** — this helps with taxes and future funding.

Step 5: Build Slowly, Not Loudly

You don't need to announce every move. Move quietly, build strong, and let your success speak for you later.

Step 6: Market Smart — Not Expensive

Use what's free:

- Social media (Instagram, Facebook, TikTok)
- WhatsApp groups
- Community boards
- Church networks
- Referrals

Word-of-mouth is still the immigrant's best marketing tool.

5. The Man Who Worked Two Jobs Until His Business Paid His Rent

Luis from El Salvador worked two jobs — construction during the day, warehouse at night.

He loved working with wood, building tables and furniture. On weekends, he'd build small pieces for friends.

He started posting his work on Facebook Marketplace. Orders began to come in slowly but steady.

After a year, his side hustle made enough to cover his rent. That's when he quit one of his jobs to focus more.

Now he has a small furniture business called **Luis Custom Woodworks.**

He said something powerful:

"I didn't chase comfort; I chased consistency."

That's the spirit of a true builder.

6. Don't Wait to Be Ready

If you're waiting to feel ready, you'll wait forever.
No one feels ready when they start, not even the most successful people you admire.

Start messy, learn fast, adjust quickly.
You'll make mistakes, yes, but those mistakes will teach you lessons no school can.

Every immigrant who ever built something started from confusion, but they kept moving.

7. Your Business Is Your Freedom Ticket

When you own something, even a small hustle, you gain *options*.
You can decide how to work, when to grow, and where to go.

That's why your job is your income, but your business is your independence.

Even if it's small at first, a food stand, a cleaning service, a T-shirt brand — build it with pride.
Because one day, that "small thing" might feed your family, hire others, and build your legacy.

8. Lessons from Silent Builders

The most successful immigrants I know rarely boast about their beginnings.

They were the ones quietly saving, planning, and learning, while others laughed or partied.

They didn't dress rich. They were *becoming* rich.

Their strength was in **patience and persistence.**

"If you can survive the first few years of struggle, the rest will start to flow."

9. Practical Tips for Immigrant Entrepreneurs

- Start small but think big.
- Learn about taxes and business deductions — they'll save you money.
- Network with other immigrant business owners.
- Don't be afraid to ask questions; local small business centers often offer free help.
- Keep learning: YouTube, podcasts, free webinars.

  Knowledge is the cheapest investment with the highest return.

10. Blueprint Summary — The Builder's Code

Start with what you have, where you are.
Focus more on execution than perfection.
Build silently, grow loudly.
Let discipline be your loudest language.
Don't chase applause — chase stability.

Final Lesson:

Immigrants are natural entrepreneurs.
We know how to survive, stretch, and multiply; that's business in its purest form.

The goal isn't just to make a living, but to **build a life**.

And when you finally own your business, even if it's small, you'll realize you didn't just build income;
you built **confidence, control, and freedom.**

Quote to End the Chapter:

"If they don't invite you to the table, bring your own chair.
And if they still don't make room, build your own table."

Chapter 7:

Ghost Mode — The Power of Focus, Silence, and Consistency

When you first arrive in a new country, everyone wants to know what you're up to.
"How's life in America?"
"Where do you work?"
"Have you bought a car yet?"

You might smile and say, "I'm working on it," but deep down, you know they're not just asking, they're *measuring*.

In the beginning, you might feel pressure to prove something, to show that you're doing well.
So you start sharing everything: your plans, your hustle, your progress.

But here's a truth every successful immigrant learns eventually:

The less you announce, the more peace you keep.

That's where *Ghost Mode* begins.

1. What Is Ghost Mode?

Ghost Mode isn't about isolation or arrogance.
It's a *mental state*, where you focus so deeply on your goals that you tune out every distraction.

It's when you stop explaining yourself, stop seeking validation, and stop trying to prove your progress.

You simply **disappear into your purpose**, working silently, saving aggressively, planning carefully, and letting results make the noise later.

Ghost Mode means:

- No unnecessary updates.
- No pressure to impress.
- No energy wasted on gossip, drama, or comparison.

It's peace over popularity.
Discipline over display.

2. Story: The Man Who Stopped Posting

Daniel, a Jamaican immigrant, used to post everything online, new shoes, new car, new apartment.
He wanted people back home to see that he was doing well.

But after a while, the pressure got heavy. Every time he hit a setback, he felt ashamed because everyone "expected" him to keep winning.

So he went quiet.

No more posts. No more updates. Just work, rest, repeat.

He focused on clearing his debts, saving money, and improving his skills.
Two years later, he didn't just "look successful"; he *was* successful.

He said something powerful:

"When I stopped performing for people, I started progressing for myself."

That's Ghost Mode, working in private until your peace and progress speak louder than your posts ever could.

3. The Science of Silence

There's real power in silence.
When you stop explaining and start executing, your brain becomes calmer, sharper, and more productive.

Noise creates distraction.
Silence creates focus.

Most people lose their edge because they waste energy trying to prove they're doing something instead of *actually doing it*.

Ghost Mode protects your energy.
It keeps your focus pure and your spirit unbothered.

4. The Power of "Disappearing to Build"

Every immigrant who became great went through a season where they "disappeared."

- They worked extra hours instead of hanging out.
- They saved instead of showing off.
- They studied while others partied.

It wasn't punishment, it was preparation.

Ghost Mode is that season when you're not visible, but you're growing roots.
The world won't see it yet, but when you finally bloom, it will make sense.

Remember:

You can't grow in public if you haven't built in private.

5. The Nurse Who Went Off the Radar

Ngozi, a nurse from Nigeria, used to attend every gathering, wedding, birthday, and dinner.
Everyone knew her as "the life of the party."

But one year, she decided to go off the radar.
She limited her outings, focused on clearing student loans, and took weekend classes to earn her BSN.

People said, "You've changed."
She just smiled and kept quiet.

Three years later, she bought her own house.
Those same people started asking her, "How did you do it?"

She said simply,

"While you were watching each other, I was watching my goals."

That's Ghost Mode in action.

6. How to Enter Ghost Mode (The Blueprint)

Here's how to intentionally enter your *season of silence and focus*:

Step 1: Identify Your Goal

Be clear about what you want. Is it saving $10,000? Finishing school? Starting a business?
Write it down and lock in.

Step 2: Cut Out Distractions

Silence doesn't mean isolation; it means *prioritization.*
Reduce social media time. Limit unnecessary outings.
Focus your energy where it multiplies.

Step 3: Move Quietly

You don't have to announce every plan.
Let progress surprise people.
Let success be your update.

Step 4: Protect Your Energy

Not everyone deserves access to you while you're building.
Distance isn't disrespect — it's self-respect.

Step 5: Stay Consistent, Even When No One's Watching

This is the hardest part — showing up when it feels invisible.
But remember: *Every silent day adds up.*

7. The Uber Driver Who Studied in His Car

Farouk, from Pakistan, drove Uber for two years while studying for his IT certification.

He didn't tell anyone.
Between rides, he studied. Late nights, he practiced coding on his laptop.

One day, he passed his exam and landed a remote tech job — tripled his income.

No one saw the nights he sacrificed.
They just saw the result.

Farouk said,

"I wasn't missing. I was mastering."

That's the Ghost Mode mindset — silent growth that leads to loud success.

8. The Discipline Behind Consistency

Ghost Mode isn't glamorous.
It's boring. Repetitive. Sometimes lonely.

But that's what makes it powerful.

Every day you stay consistent, even when no one claps, you build strength.
Discipline is the real success currency.

Don't confuse excitement with progress.
Progress is quiet, steady, and patient.

9. Your "Ghost Season" Is Temporary

Ghost Mode doesn't mean hiding forever.
It's a season — a time to build your foundation so that when you reappear, you're stronger, stable, and ready.

Like seeds underground — unseen but preparing to break through.

When your time comes, you won't need to announce it.
Your results will speak for you.

10. Blueprint Summary — The Ghost Mode Code

Focus more on your grind than your image.
Talk less, do more.
Don't seek validation — seek progress.
Protect your peace; it's your power source.
Stay consistent until your results become undeniable.

Final Lesson:

In a world where everyone wants to be seen, Ghost Mode is your advantage.
Because while they're performing, you're *becoming*.

When you reappear, you won't need to explain yourself — your success will introduce you.

Quote to End the Chapter:

"Don't tell them what you're building.
Show them when it's done."

Chapter 8:

Dare to Be Great — Breaking Fear, Thinking Bold, and Owning Your Space

When you've lived in survival mode for a long time, success can feel strange.
Many immigrants know that feeling — the quiet fear of wanting more but worrying that they might not *deserve* more.

You tell yourself:
"I just want a simple life."
But deep down, there's a louder voice whispering,

"You were meant for more than survival."

That whisper is the beginning of greatness.

1. The Fear That Follows You

When you land in a new country, you carry more than your luggage.
You carry fear — fear of failing, fear of being judged, fear of starting over.

You think of your accent, your background, your limited network, and that voice in your head says,
"Stay small. Don't draw attention. Just blend in."

But blending in has never built legends.

If you want to create something different, a business, a brand, a new path, you must first confront that inner fear that keeps you quiet.

2. The Woman Who Refused to Play Small

Ada moved to the U.S. from Nigeria with a nursing degree. For years, she worked night shifts, always tired, always saving.

But she had another dream, to start a small skincare line using African herbs and oils her grandmother taught her about.

She kept saying, "One day."
Then one day became three years.

Finally, after losing her job during the pandemic, she decided to *start scared.*
She mixed oils in her kitchen, designed labels on Canva, and sold her first 10 jars online.

Today, her products are in three local beauty stores.

When asked what changed, she said,

"Fear never left me. I just stopped letting it drive."

That's what it means to **dare to be great** — to act even when your hands are shaking.

3. Greatness Requires Permission — Yours

No one is going to call you one morning and say,
"Congratulations, it's your turn to be great."

You have to *decide it for yourself.*

Greatness starts the day you stop waiting for validation.
When you give yourself permission to dream, to build, to try, to fail, and to try again.

If you keep waiting for the perfect time, it'll never come.
There's no perfect time — only a bold decision.

4. Story: The Delivery Driver Who Thought Like a Boss

Ravi, from India, delivered packages for a living.
Every day, he drove through neighborhoods full of successful business owners.

One day, he asked himself,
"What if I stopped being the delivery guy, and started being the one who *hires* delivery guys?"

He saved $200 every week for a year, learned e-commerce through YouTube, and started his own online gadget store.

It didn't blow up overnight.
But after 18 months, his side hustle replaced his delivery job.

Ravi said something powerful:

"The biggest shift wasn't in my income. It was in my identity."

He stopped thinking like an employee.
He started thinking like a boss.

That's what happens when you dare to be great — your world expands to match your mindset.

5. The Immigrant Advantage

Many immigrants see their background as a disadvantage.
But here's the truth: it's your *superpower*.

You already know how to start from zero.
You already know how to survive uncertainty.
You already know how to build something from nothing.

That's what most people fear — but you've done it before.

So imagine what happens when you combine that resilience with bold thinking.
You stop just surviving in a foreign land… and start *dominating*.

6. The Enemy Called Comparison

In this digital age, it's easy to scroll online and feel behind.
Someone just bought a house.
Another one launched a business.
Another posted a "soft life" vacation in Bali.

You start questioning yourself:
"What am I doing wrong?"

But here's the truth:
You're not behind — you're just on a different route.

Comparison kills creativity.
It makes you chase someone else's version of success instead of defining your own.

Stay in your lane.
Run your race.
You're not late — you're *becoming*.

7. The Man Who Took the Long Road

Juan, from El Salvador, came to the U.S. and worked construction for years.
While others laughed at his slow progress, he kept saving, taking online English classes, and volunteering to help manage project budgets.

Five years later, that experience helped him land a project coordinator role.

He said,

"My road was slow, but it was solid."

He dared to be great — not by rushing, but by staying faithful to his process.

8. How to Dare to Be Great (The Practical Blueprint)

Step 1: Redefine Success for *You*

Forget social media's version of success.
Ask yourself: "What does a great life mean *to me*?"
Write it down. Own it.

Step 2: Start Scared, but Start Anyway

Fear will never fully leave. Start with shaking hands if you must.
Courage isn't the absence of fear — it's progress in spite of it.

Step 3: Invest in Yourself

Buy the course. Attend the seminar. Learn the skill.
You are your best investment.

Step 4: Think Like a Creator

Stop thinking only about "getting a job."
Ask: "What can I *create*? What value can I offer?"

Step 5: Surround Yourself With Growth

Your circle should push you, not pacify you.
If everyone around you is comfortable, you're in the wrong circle.

9. The Bold Barber

Efe came from Ghana with nothing but his clippers.
He started cutting hair in a friend's garage.

Instead of complaining about slow days, he studied business videos at night.
Within two years, he opened a small shop.
Then he hired two other barbers.
Now, he runs a full grooming studio with his name on the door.

He said,

"At first, I just wanted to make ends meet.
Now, I make decisions."

That's the reward of daring to be great — you don't just work in a system, you *build* one.

10. The Boldness Blueprint — Mindset Shifts

Stop apologizing for your dreams.
Don't shrink your goals to fit your fear.
Take risks — small but consistent ones.
Own your accent, your roots, your story — that's your brand.
Believe that you belong in every room your hard work takes you to.

11. Closing Message: Your Name Deserves to Be Remembered

There's a generation coming after you — your kids, your siblings, your community.
They need to *see* someone who dared to be great, so they can believe it's possible too.

Every immigrant who rises sends a message back home:

"You can make it too."

So stop hiding behind modesty.
You've sacrificed too much to play small.
You came too far to only go halfway.

Dare to be great — loudly, boldly, fearlessly.
Because the world needs your version of success.

Quote to End the Chapter:

"Your fear is loud because your purpose is big.
Step forward anyway — greatness is waiting on the other side."

Chapter 9:

Financial Freedom — Mastering Money, Credit, and Discipline as an Immigrant

When you first arrive in the U.S., money disappears faster than you expect.
You think you're earning a lot, until you realize rent, taxes, insurance, groceries, and remittances are waiting at the door.

Then come the credit cards.
At first, they feel like a blessing, until you wake up one morning and realize your balance is higher than your paycheck.

That's when it hits you:
It's not how much you earn that makes you free — it's **how well you manage it.**

1. The Immigrant Money Trap

Most immigrants start with a simple dream: *"Let me just make enough."*
But that mindset can keep you trapped forever — working hard, earning well, but never truly *free*.

Why? Because nobody teaches you the *system* behind money in America.
You learn by trial and error — and those errors are expensive.

The truth is, financial freedom isn't about luck or income level.
It's about habits, awareness, and control.

If you don't tell your money where to go, it will tell you where you can't.

2. The Nurse Who Made $90K and Still Struggled

Maria, a Filipino nurse, earned nearly $90,000 a year.
Yet, she constantly felt broke.

Every month, after bills, she sent money home, paid off debts, and treated herself a little — because "I deserve it."
But she never tracked her spending.

After three years, she realized she had *nothing saved.*

So she made one small change — she started budgeting every dollar, tracking her credit score, and automating her savings.

Two years later, she had paid off $15,000 in debt and bought her first home.

She said,

"I stopped working *for* my money and started making it work *for* me."

3. The Mindset Shift: From Hustler to Wealth Builder

As immigrants, we're trained to *hustle*, take every shift, every gig, every opportunity.
But hustling without strategy leads to exhaustion, not wealth.

Financial freedom starts when you shift your thinking from:

"How much can I make?"
to
"How much can I keep, grow, and multiply?"

Working hard is good.
But working smart with your money is better.

4. Understanding the U.S. Financial Game

America runs on **credit, discipline, and records.**
If you learn how to play that game, you'll always be ahead.

Here's what you need to master:

Credit Score

It's not just a number — it's your financial passport.
It determines if you can buy a house, lease a car, or even get a business loan.
Pay on time, keep credit utilization below 30%, and avoid opening too many accounts at once.

Budgeting

Think of budgeting as freedom, not punishment.
It's how you tell your money where to go instead of wondering where it went.

Use the **50/30/20 rule**:

- 50% for needs (rent, bills, food)
- 30% for wants (fun, lifestyle)
- 20% for savings and debt repayment

Emergency Fund

Life happens — medical bills, job loss, car breakdowns.
Have at least **3–6 months of expenses** saved in a separate account.

Investing

Even small investments matter.
You can start with index funds, retirement accounts (like 401k or IRA), or even small business ventures.

5. The Uber Driver Who Bought His First House

Abdi, from Ethiopia, drove Uber for four years.
Every month, he saved $500 consistently, no matter how small his earnings were.

He learned about credit, built it up, and avoided unnecessary debt.
By year five, he had a credit score of 760 and $25,000 saved.

With that, he bought his first duplex — living in one unit, renting the other.

He said proudly,

"That house paid my rent while I was still working. That's freedom."

He didn't need a miracle — just patience and planning.

6. The Discipline of "Living Below Your Shine"

Many immigrants fall into a quiet trap — the need to *look* *successful* before actually *being* successful.

You've seen it: designer clothes, fancy cars, constant parties.
It's not bad to enjoy yourself — but not at the cost of your goals.

Learn to "live below your shine."

Let your growth be visible in your peace, not your possessions.
While others post lifestyle, you build legacy.

Remember:

Every dollar you save today is a brick in your future freedom.

7. The Couple Who Built Quiet Wealth

Olu and Tola, a Nigerian couple, lived in a modest apartment for years even after both started earning six figures.
They kept their expenses low, saved aggressively, and invested in rental properties.

Their friends teased them:
"You people are too stingy!"

But five years later, they owned three houses and had no debt.

They laughed and said,

"We weren't stingy. We were strategic."

That's what financial freedom looks like — quiet wealth, not loud stress.

8. The Immigrant's Financial Blueprint

Here's a simple plan to start mastering your money in America:

Step 1: Track Every Dollar

Write it down or use budgeting apps (like Mint, YNAB, or EveryDollar).
Awareness is step one to control.

Step 2: Build an Emergency Fund

Start small — even $50/month counts.
Consistency matters more than size.

Step 3: Build and Protect Your Credit

Pay all bills on time.
Use credit cards wisely.
Check your credit report regularly (Credit Karma, Experian).

Step 4: Eliminate Debt Slowly but Surely

Start with the **Snowball Method** — pay off smallest debts first to build momentum.

Step 5: Automate Savings and Investments

Treat your savings like a bill — non-negotiable.

Step 6: Learn and Invest

Educate yourself. Attend free financial literacy workshops or follow immigrant finance communities online.

9. The Long Game: Build for the Future, Not the Weekend

Financial freedom takes time.
It's not sexy, it's not instant — but it's *secure.*

The people who seem ahead today might be in debt tomorrow.
But the one who's building quietly, saving patiently, and planning wisely will always win in the long run.

You're not in competition with anyone — only with your old financial habits.

10. Story: The Immigrant Who Built a Legacy

Amara, from Kenya, started working in housekeeping.
She saved, learned, and started investing in small land back home while also saving in the U.S.

Ten years later, she owned property in both countries.
She sent her kids to school debt-free.

She said,

"The goal wasn't to look rich. The goal was to *never struggle again.*"

That's true financial freedom — peace, not pressure.

11. The Freedom Equation

Financial Freedom = Mindset + Management + Consistency.

It's not magic. It's mastery.

You don't need to earn six figures, you just need to manage the five you have with intention.
And when you learn that discipline, your wealth begins to multiply.

12. The Quiet Confidence of Financial Independence

There's a deep peace that comes when you no longer live paycheck to paycheck.
When your bills are paid, your savings are growing, and your future feels secure, your confidence changes.

You walk differently. You think differently. You dream differently.

That's the true reward of mastering your money:
Freedom. Not to escape your life, but to design it.

Quote to End the Chapter:

"Your first real investment isn't in stocks or property; it's in learning how to handle money like someone who plans to be free."

Chapter 10:

Building Your Business in a New Land — From Side Hustle to Structure

For many immigrants, the dream isn't just to make money, it's to make *something that lasts.*
Something with your name on it.
Something that can feed others, not just yourself.

But here's the truth most people won't say out loud:
Starting a business in a new country is scary.
The system feels complicated. The rules seem confusing. The fear of failure whispers in your ear every night.

And yet… the most successful immigrants you see today all started with the same question you have now:

"Can I really do this here?"

Yes — you can.
And you should.

Because the path to true freedom is not just earning but **owning.**

1. Why Every Immigrant Should Think Like an Owner

Jobs pay the bills.
Ownership builds the future.

When you rely on a paycheck, your income depends on someone else's decision.
When you build something of your own, even small, you start controlling your destiny.

It could be:

- A cleaning service
- A catering business
- A trucking company
- A fashion brand
- An online store
- A consulting or care agency

It doesn't matter where you start — what matters is that you *start*.

2. The Cleaner Who Became a CEO

Lina, from Haiti, worked as a cleaner for five years.
Every week, she noticed that clients were paying $250 for services she got paid $80 to deliver.

One day, she realized — she could do the same thing, legally and properly.
She registered a small business, bought supplies, and started taking small private clients.

She built a team of two, then five, then ten.
Within four years, she owned a cleaning company that employed over 20 people.

Lina said,

"America rewards people who take initiative, not just orders."

That's the immigrant blueprint — learning the system, then owning your space in it.

3. From Side Hustle to Structure

Many of us already have businesses — we just don't call them that yet.
You might braid hair, bake pastries, fix cars, or resell clothes.
That's a *hustle* — and it's powerful.

But to grow, you must structure it.

When you register your business, you unlock access to:
Business bank accounts
Credit and loans
Legal protection
Tax advantages
Trust and credibility

It's not just paperwork — it's **proof that you belong in the marketplace.**

4. How to Start a Business in America (Step by Step)

Here's how to turn your idea into something real:

Step 1: Choose Your Business Name and Type

Decide on a name that represents your brand.
Choose your structure — most immigrants start with:

- **LLC (Limited Liability Company)** for flexibility and protection.
- **Sole Proprietorship** if you're testing the waters.

Step 2: Register It

You can register your LLC with your state's Secretary of State website (usually under $200).
Some states allow online filing in minutes.

Step 3: Get an EIN (Employer Identification Number)

This is your business's Social Security number — used for taxes and banking.
You can get it free from the **IRS website**.

Step 4: Open a Business Bank Account

Keep your personal and business money separate.
It helps with taxes, credit, and professionalism.

Step 5: Get the Right Licenses/Permits

Depending on your business type (cleaning, food, trucking, care), check your city or state's small business office for required permits.

Step 6: Build a Simple Brand

You don't need a fancy logo just a name, purpose, and professionalism.
A clean logo, Gmail business email, and maybe a one-page website is enough to start.

Step 7: Market Yourself Smartly

Start small — referrals, social media, community pages, church networks.
Be consistent. Reliability builds reputation faster than ads.

5. The Delivery Guy Who Created a Logistics Brand

Mohammed, from Sudan, started delivering packages for Amazon Flex.
He noticed delivery demand was always high.

So he formed his own LLC, leased two vans, and partnered with local stores for deliveries.

Within two years, he had three contracts and six employees.

He said,

"At first, I was scared to register my company; I thought it was too complicated.
Then I realized it's just paperwork. The real work is showing up daily."

6. The Power of Documentation

In America, **documentation is your currency.**
Whether you're applying for a grant, contract, or loan — the system doesn't care how hard you work; it cares how well you document.

Keep these simple but powerful records:

- Bank statements
- Invoices

- Tax returns
- Receipts
- Business registration and EIN

These papers are not just documents — they are your *proof of growth*.

7. The Barber Who Built a Brand

Kwame, from Ghana, started cutting hair in his cousin's basement.
He was good — talented, loyal clients.

But every year, he stayed stuck because he never registered officially.

One day, a city inspector warned him to formalize or shut down. He took that advice seriously, registered his business, and rented a small suite.

Within three years, *Kwame Cuts* became a registered brand — he hired barbers, started selling his own beard oil, and signed a commercial lease.

He said,

"That one paper, my business registration, changed how the city treated me, how banks treated me, and how I saw myself."

That's ownership.

8. Common Fears Immigrants Face (and How to Overcome Them)

"I don't know how to start."

Learn and ask questions.
Every city has a *Small Business Development Center (SBDC)* — free training and guidance for new entrepreneurs.

"What if I fail?"

You will fail — a few times.
But each failure is tuition for success.

"I don't have the money."

Start small.
Use what you have. Many great businesses started with less than $500 — just consistency and creativity.

"My English isn't perfect."

Your service can speak for you.
Excellence doesn't need accent approval.

9. The Babysitter Who Built a Care Agency

Sofia, from Colombia, worked as a nanny for seven years. She loved the work but felt capped.

She took a business course online, registered a small LLC, and began connecting other qualified caregivers to families.

Two years later, she owned a small care agency, hired staff, and earned more by managing others than she ever did working alone.

She said,

"My dream didn't need permission — it just needed structure."

10. Thinking Like a Boss

When you become a business owner, you stop asking "Can I afford this?" and start asking "How can I create this?"

Bosses think in systems, not shifts.
They see opportunity in every challenge.

The truth is, immigrants already have the perfect foundation for entrepreneurship — work ethic, humility, adaptability, and hunger.
All you need now is *direction*.

11. Business Credit and Growth

Once your business is structured, build **business credit.**
It helps you separate personal finances and prepare for future scaling.

Start with:

- A business checking account
- An EIN
- A D-U-N-S number (from Dun & Bradstreet)
- Small business credit cards or vendor accounts

Pay on time, keep utilization low, and your business credit will grow — opening doors to loans, leases, and government contracts.

12. Story: The Man Who Started With One Truck

Ade, from Nigeria, saved up for one used box truck.
He got a DOT number, insurance, and registered as an LLC.

He drove himself for a year. Then he hired another driver.
Three years later, he owned five trucks and was bidding for state logistics contracts.

When asked how he did it, he said,

"I stopped thinking like an immigrant — I started thinking like an investor."

That's the shift this chapter is all about.

13. The Ownership Blueprint

Start small but start smart.
Register your business early.
Keep your records clean.
Treat your clients like kings.
Keep learning — attend workshops, network, and study others in your field.

You don't need a million dollars to start, you need a million dollars' worth of **discipline and clarity.**

14. Closing Message: From Worker to Founder

You didn't cross oceans and borders just to survive.
You came to build, to rise, to create something that carries your name and your values.

Every immigrant who becomes an owner sends a powerful message:

"We are not just here to take jobs — we are here to create them."

When your name is on that registration paper, your children will know that you didn't just live in America — you *built* in America.

Quote to End the Chapter:

"Don't wait for permission to build.
Start where you are, use what you have, and grow what you own."

Chapter 11:

Networking and Building Community — The Power of Relationships in a New Country

When you first arrive in a new country, silence can feel louder than anything else.

You walk into stores and no one knows your name.

You go to work, keep your head down, and go home to an empty room that echoes with thoughts.

You begin to miss the random hellos, the street greetings, the laughter of home.

And you start to realize — success in this new land isn't just about *what* you know.

It's also about *who* you know.

And more importantly, *who knows you.*

1. The Silent Struggle of Starting Over

Every immigrant knows this feeling: you leave a place where you were *somebody* and arrive in a place where you're *nobody.*

Back home, people knew your family name.

Your accent didn't need explaining.

Here, you're just "the new one."

But that's where the magic begins, because in every new land, you have the chance to *redefine* yourself.
You can build a new name, a new tribe, and a new legacy.

2. The Woman Who Found Her Tribe at a Church Potluck

Maria moved from Brazil to Houston with no family, no network, and no car.
She worked long shifts as a caregiver, saving every dollar.

One Sunday, she accepted an invitation to a small church potluck.
That day changed everything.

She met a woman who owned a cleaning business, who later became her mentor.
Within months, Maria joined her company, learned the ropes, and later started her own team.

Maria says,

"I thought success would come from working harder.
But it came faster when I started *connecting smarter.*"

That's the secret many immigrants overlook — your next opportunity is often one handshake away.

3. Why Relationships Are the Real Currency

Money is important.
But relationships are wealth that never runs out.

Every recommendation, every new client, every chance to grow often comes through *someone who trusts you.*

In a new country, you build wealth not just through effort but through **connection.**

A strong network can help you:

- Find jobs or contracts faster
- Get business advice
- Access community resources
- Feel emotionally supported
- Avoid costly mistakes others already made

4. Building Your Network, Step by Step

Step 1: Start with Common Ground

Join spaces where people already share something with you, your language, faith, profession, or passion.

- Community or cultural centers
- Churches, mosques, or temples
- Immigrant associations
- Online groups for newcomers

Start where you're *understood and* then grow outward.

Step 2: Give Before You Ask

The best way to build trust is to be valuable.
Offer help, share information, and show up consistently.
People remember kindness longer than requests.

Step 3: Learn to Introduce Yourself With Confidence

You don't need a fancy title.
You just need clarity.
Say:

"Hi, my name is Shola. I work in construction estimating, and I help companies plan their projects better."

Simple. Clear. Memorable.

Step 4: Attend Networking Events — Even When You Feel Out of Place

Yes, it's uncomfortable at first.
You'll feel like the quiet one in a room of confident speakers.
But remember: every "successful" person there once felt the same way.

The more you show up, the more you become *seen.*
And in this country, visibility creates opportunity.

5. Story: The Uber Driver Who Became a Realtor

Adebayo from Nigeria drove Uber for two years.
Every day, he spoke with passengers — entrepreneurs, realtors, small business owners.

Instead of just driving in silence, he asked questions.
He took notes.
He built connections.

One day, a passenger told him, "You'd make a great real estate agent."

That one sentence changed everything.
He got his real estate license, joined a brokerage, and two years later, Adebayo was no longer just driving people to destinations; he was helping them *buy* their destinations.

He said,

"Talking to people turned my steering wheel into a microphone for opportunity."

6. The Power of Mentorship

Every successful immigrant stands on the shoulders of someone who showed them the way.

A mentor is not always a big CEO or a famous name — sometimes it's a neighbor, a manager, or a community elder who simply believes in you.

Mentorship gives you shortcuts.
You learn through guidance, not just mistakes.

Tip: Don't wait for a mentor to find you.
Ask. Observe. Offer to help.

Sometimes mentorship begins when you say,

"I admire how you've done this, can you teach me how you started?"

7. The Teen Who Found Family Through Volunteering

Kofi moved to Boston at 18, lost and homesick.
He started volunteering at a food pantry every Saturday.

Within months, he had friends, job leads, and a sense of belonging he hadn't felt since Ghana.

Volunteering gave him *visibility and value* and through it, he built relationships that later helped him get his first apartment and job.

He said,

"When you serve, people see your heart before your accent."

8. How to Build Relationships That Last

Relationships don't grow by accident — they grow by *attention*. Here's how:

Follow up. Don't just collect contacts; connect with them.
Be reliable. People trust those who do what they say.
Celebrate others. Congratulate, encourage, and uplift.
Stay humble. Success should make you approachable, not unreachable.

The people you treat well when you have nothing will often become your strongest allies when you have something.

9. Community Is Protection

In a foreign land, community is not just emotional — it's *practical.*

Your network can:

- Alert you to new laws or programs
- Help with job leads
- Offer referrals for housing or legal help
- Support you during emergencies

No one thrives alone.

Even the most independent immigrant still needs people to call in the middle of the night when life gets real.

10. The Woman Who Built a Business from WhatsApp Groups

Fatima, from Pakistan, started selling homemade snacks in her neighborhood.
She joined a local WhatsApp moms' group and started sharing pictures.

Orders began to roll in, then referrals.
She turned her kitchen hustle into a registered catering business.

Her network didn't just buy from her — they *believed* in her.

Fatima said,

"I didn't have marketing, I had people.
And people can take your business farther than ads ever can."

11. How to Network Without Losing Yourself

Sometimes networking can feel fake — like everyone's pretending to smile and trade business cards.
But real networking isn't about pretending.

It's about showing up *authentically.*
You don't need to sound American. You don't need perfect grammar.
You just need genuine interest in people.

Ask questions. Listen more than you talk. Remember names.

People may forget your accent, but they'll never forget how you made them feel.

12. Building a Circle That Elevates You

There are two kinds of circles:

- The ones that keep you comfortable.
- And the ones that push you to grow.

Choose the second.

Surround yourself with people who talk about progress, not gossip.
Who celebrate your wins, not compete with them.
Who remind you of your dreams when you forget them yourself.

13. The Accountant Who Found Success Through a Network

Chinedu, a trained accountant from Nigeria, couldn't get hired at first.
He joined a local African professionals' group in Massachusetts.

Through that group, he met someone who connected him with a small firm looking for a junior accountant.
He got hired.
Two years later, he was promoted.

He said,

"My degree didn't open that door, my community did."

14. Turning Connections into Collaboration

When you meet people, think beyond friendship, think partnership.

Can you start a small business together?
Can you refer clients to each other?
Can you share knowledge, tools, or space?

That's how immigrant communities grow wealth, through *collaboration, not competition.*

15. Closing Message: You're Never Alone

Every connection you build is a bridge.
And the more bridges you build, the further you can go.

You left your homeland, but you didn't leave your humanity.
People still need your smile, your energy, your ideas, your courage.

The truth is — your community is already waiting for you.
You just have to show up and say,

"Hi, my name is [your name]. I'm new here — but I'm ready to grow."

Quote to End the Chapter:

"Your network is not just who you know, it's who believes in your dream when you start doubting it yourself."

Chapter 12:

The Emotional Journey — Handling Homesickness, Pressure, and Self-Doubt

No one talks enough about *the quiet parts* of being an immigrant.

The nights when you cry silently after a phone call from home. The moments when you smile in public but feel invisible inside. The pressure to "make it" — even when you're barely holding it together.

Behind every smiling immigrant photo on social media is a heart that has battled loneliness, fear, and doubt, and still chooses to keep going.

This chapter is for that heart.

1. The Weight of Leaving Everything Behind

When you leave your home country, you don't just leave behind a location — you leave behind your *identity.*

Back home, you knew every street, every accent, every joke. Here, you start again — explaining your name, your accent, your story.

At first, you feel brave.
Then, reality starts to whisper:

"Can I really do this?"
"What if I fail?"

But what most people forget is, *you've already done something extraordinary.*
You left your comfort zone to chase a dream.
That courage alone puts you in the top 1%.

2. The First Winter

When Ahmed moved from Sudan to Minnesota, his first winter broke him.

He had never seen snow before.
His shoes soaked through. His car wouldn't start. He walked to work freezing, exhausted, and homesick.

One night, he sat in his tiny apartment and whispered,

"Maybe I made a mistake."

But then he remembered his mother's last words before he left:

"The road will not welcome you kindly but walk it with faith."

Years later, when Ahmed became a mechanical engineer, he said,

"Every time I see snow now, I smile. Because I survived the season that almost made me quit."

That's the immigrant journey: you survive the storms others couldn't stand in.

3. The Pressure to Succeed

Every immigrant carries an invisible backpack of expectations.

Your family calls you *"our hope."*
Friends back home say, *"You're lucky to be in America."*

So you keep working — harder, longer, without rest, because you feel like your success isn't just yours; it's for everyone who believed in you.

But the truth is, **you can't pour from an empty cup.**

Success means nothing if you lose yourself in the process.
You have a right to rest. To breathe. To say, *"I'm trying."*

You don't owe anyone perfection, just progress.

4. The Comparison Trap

Social media can be dangerous when you're far from home.
You see your friends back home building houses or getting married.
You see others in the U.S. buying cars, posting vacations, living "soft life."

You start to feel like you're behind.

But here's the truth, **everyone's journey is timed differently.**
Some are in their planting season.
Others are in their harvest.

Don't compare your Chapter 1 to someone's Chapter 10.

Your story is still being written, and some of the most beautiful pages take the longest to form.

5. The Girl Who Wanted to Go Home

Lydia came from Kenya to study nursing in Ohio.
By her second semester, she wanted to quit.
Her English wasn't fluent, she failed a class, and she missed her family.

One day, she called her father crying.
"I'm not smart enough," she said.

Her father replied softly,

"You are smart enough, you're just in a new language."

Those words changed everything.
She started studying harder, joined a study group, and practiced English by reading children's books aloud.

Today, Lydia is a registered nurse helping new immigrants find housing and scholarships.

Sometimes, your pain becomes your purpose if you keep going long enough to see it transform.

6. Homesickness Is Real — and Normal

It's okay to miss home.
To miss your mother's cooking, your native language, your people.
That doesn't make you weak, it makes you *human*.

Here's how to ease the ache:

 Call home regularly, but not every time you're sad.
 Create new traditions in your new country.

Cook your native food and share it with others.
Celebrate your culture instead of hiding it.

You're not losing your roots, you're expanding them.

7. The Man Who Found Home in His Kitchen

Pedro from Mexico used to feel lonely after moving to Chicago. So every Sunday, he cooked his grandmother's recipes and invited neighbors over.

That small act turned strangers into friends.
His kitchen became his comfort, his new version of *home*.

He says,

"I stopped waiting to feel at home, I started creating it."

That's the power of belonging; it begins with what you build around you.

8. Handling Self-Doubt

There will be moments when you question yourself:

"Am I enough?"
"Do I belong here?"

You'll doubt your accent, your experience, your dreams.

But self-doubt isn't a sign you're failing, it's proof that you're stretching beyond your limits.

Courage doesn't mean you don't feel fear.
It means you move *despite* it.

Remember: even the most confident people you see once felt exactly like you do.

9. How to Stay Mentally Strong

Here are practical habits that keep your spirit healthy:

1. **Journal often.** Write how you feel, it helps you release emotions.
2. **Exercise and eat well.** Your body and mind are connected.
3. **Talk to someone.** Find a trusted friend, mentor, or counselor.
4. **Celebrate small wins.** Every step forward counts.
5. **Pray, meditate, or stay spiritually grounded.** Faith gives meaning to the struggle.

You're not weak for seeking help, you're wise for choosing healing.

10. Story: The Taxi Driver Who Found Peace

Samuel from Ghana drove 10-hour shifts daily in New York City. One day, after a long ride, a passenger left behind a small book titled *"The Power of Now."*

He started reading it between trips — and it changed how he saw life.

Instead of worrying about the future, he began focusing on one day at a time.

He said,

"I stopped rushing to arrive. I started living where I am."

That's emotional freedom — peace in the present.

11. The Strength Behind the Struggle

Every challenge you've faced, language barriers, racism, rejection, exhaustion, is quietly building your resilience.

You're not just surviving, you're transforming.

One day, you'll look back and realize:
The version of you that landed at the airport scared and uncertain — became the version that built a new life from scratch.

That's strength beyond measure.

12. When It Feels Like Nobody Understands

Sometimes you'll feel invisible, like nobody sees your effort or your pain.
But even when no one claps, *keep going.*

You are writing a story that one day will inspire someone else to begin.

Your courage today is someone's hope tomorrow.

13. The Immigrant Who Became a Therapist

Aisha moved from Pakistan to the U.S. as a teenager.
She faced bullying for her accent and isolation at school.

Years later, she studied psychology to help others feel less alone. Today, she runs a counseling center for immigrants — offering therapy in multiple languages.

Her pain became her mission.

She says,

"I couldn't find a safe space, so I built one."

That's what immigrants do. We turn struggle into service.

14. You Are More Than Your Status

Your visa status doesn't define your value.
Your accent doesn't limit your intelligence.
Your background doesn't determine your destiny.

You're not "just an immigrant."
You're an investor in your future.
A pioneer.
A bridge-builder.

Every day you show up and try, you're already winning.

15. Closing Message: You Belong Here

Never forget this:
You belong here.
Your dreams are valid.
Your effort matters.

You didn't come this far to only come this far.

So, take a deep breath, lift your head, and whisper to yourself:

"I am still becoming everything I was meant to be."

And you are.

Quote to End the Chapter:

"Home isn't always a place. Sometimes it's the peace you build within yourself when you realize you made it through what tried to break you."

Chapter 13:

The Immigrant Entrepreneur — Turning Hustle Into Legacy

Every immigrant starts with a hustle.
Driving Uber. Doing hair. Selling food. Cleaning offices.

It begins as a way to survive, but if you're wise, it can become your way to *thrive*.

Because one day you'll realize:
You don't just have to work for opportunity…
You can **create** it.

1. From Employee Mindset to Entrepreneur Mindset

Most of us were taught:

"Go to school, get a job, and be safe."

That's good advice, until you realize the system wasn't designed to make you *free*

A job can feed you.
A business can feed generations.

The goal isn't to quit your job tomorrow.
It's to start thinking like a *builder*, even while you're still working.

Entrepreneurship isn't about owning a company; it's about **owning your decisions.**

2. From Cleaner to Company Owner

Blessing, a Ghanaian woman in Maryland, started as a janitor.
She worked nights cleaning office buildings, earning $14/hour.

But instead of complaining, she observed how contracts worked, what clients wanted, what products were used.

After two years, she registered her own cleaning company.
At first, she got small jobs — cleaning homes, salons, small offices.

By year five, she had 12 employees.
By year seven, she had contracts with hospitals.

She said,

"America gave me the same broom. I just decided to own it."

That's the mindset shift — from worker to owner.

3. The Immigrant Advantage

Immigrants are built for business.
We already know how to adapt, work hard, and stretch a dollar.

We take risks daily just by living here.
We understand sacrifice and long-term vision.

Those same traits — discipline, endurance, and creativity — are the foundation of entrepreneurship.

You don't need perfect English, perfect timing, or perfect capital.
You just need to start with what you have and grow from there.

4. Start Small, Start Smart

You don't need $50,000 to start.
You need *clarity* and *consistency*.

Here's how to begin:

1. **Identify your skill or passion.**
   What do people already pay you for or praise you for?
   (Cooking, photography, repairs, design, cleaning, tutoring, nails, etc.)

2. **Start where you are.**
   Begin from your home, car, or online.

3. **Register your business.**
   Get an LLC or sole proprietorship — it builds credibility and protects you legally.

4. **Open a business bank account.**
   Never mix personal and business money.

5. **Keep records.**
   Use apps or simple notebooks to track expenses and income.

6. **Learn taxes and deductions.**
   Many small business owners lose money simply by not knowing what they can write off.

5. The Uber Driver Who Built a Logistics Company

When Temitope from Nigeria bought his first car for Uber, he thought it was just a hustle.
But he paid attention, learned about dispatching, routes, and how delivery companies worked.

He added a second car, then a third.
Within four years, he registered a logistics company, got contracts with small businesses, and hired other drivers.

Today, he employs six people — including other immigrants who once struggled like him.

He said,

"I stopped asking for opportunity and started building it."

6. Your Hustle Is a Seed

No matter how small your side hustle looks, treat it with *respect*.

- If you cook for friends, brand it.
- If you braid hair, create a name card.
- If you clean homes, create invoices and collect reviews.

Professionalism turns your side hustle into a *real business*.

7. The Fear Factor

The biggest reason many immigrants don't start businesses is **fear.**

Fear of failure.
Fear of language barriers.
Fear of "what will people say?"

But here's the truth:
You already faced the hardest fear, *starting over in a foreign country.*

If you can survive that, you can survive starting a business.

8. The Man Who Sold Snacks to Build a Store

Manuel from El Salvador started selling homemade snacks outside construction sites.
He saved every dollar, reinvested, and built relationships with workers who loved his food.

Five years later, he opened a small grocery store — "Manuel's Market."
Now, he employs others, including his two brothers who later joined him in the U.S.

He says,

"I didn't build a store, I built a bridge for my family."

That's legacy.

9. Learning the System

Entrepreneurship in the U.S. is *structured.*
Once you understand the system, it becomes your playground.

Here's what you should know early:

- **Get an EIN (Employer Identification Number)** free from IRS.gov.

- **Register your business** at the state level.

- **Keep your receipts** for tax deductions.

- **Learn about business credit** — yes, your business can have its own credit score!

- **Network with other small business owners.**

  You don't have to figure it out alone — there are free resources like:

- SBA (Small Business Administration)

- SCORE (mentorship for small businesses)

- Local immigrant entrepreneurship programs and grants

10. The Tailor Who Became a Brand

Mariam from Sierra Leone used to sew clothes from her apartment for extra income.
She posted her designs online and received a few local orders.

Instead of stopping there, she branded herself, started a small Instagram page, and asked happy customers to post photos.

> Within a year, she had 5,000 followers and steady weekend orders.
> Now, she has a studio — "Mariam Designs."

> She said,

"I stopped being just a tailor. I became a storyteller through fabric."

11. The Power of Multiple Streams

One income is survival.
Multiple incomes are freedom.

The average millionaire has *seven* income streams — and most started with just one hustle that grew.

As an immigrant, you can:

- Keep your job while running a side hustle
- Invest small in real estate or stocks
- Build an online business or service
- Create digital products or tutoring gigs

You don't have to do it all, just do *something* that earns while you sleep.

12. The Legacy Mindset

You didn't come to this country just to pay bills and die tired.
You came to *build something that outlives you.*

That's what legacy means — leaving footprints that guide others.

Maybe your children won't have to struggle like you did.
Maybe your story will give courage to someone still afraid to begin.

You don't need to be rich to build a legacy, you just need to be intentional.

13. Story: The Family That Turned Pain Into Purpose

After losing his job during the pandemic, Emmanuel from Haiti and his wife began cooking from home, selling Haitian meals to neighbors.

They called it "Taste of Port-au-Prince."

Word spread. Orders grew.
They bought a small food truck.

Now, they cater events and employ two other immigrants.

Emmanuel said,

"I didn't lose my job, I found my calling."

That's the immigrant spirit — turning crisis into creation.

14. The Importance of Visibility

Don't hide your business out of fear or shyness.
Promote it with pride.

Use social media wisely — let your work speak for you.
Register on Google Business, collect reviews, and tell your story.

People don't just buy products; they buy *purpose.*
Let them see yours.

15. Closing Message: Build It Boldly

You've already proven your courage by moving to a new country. Now prove your greatness by building something that carries your name with pride.

Start small.
Grow slow.
But stay consistent.

Because one day, you'll look back and realize — what started as a hustle became your *legacy*.

Quote to End the Chapter:

"The immigrant doesn't just chase dreams, they build them with bare hands, brave hearts, and borrowed time."

Chapter 14:

Building a Legacy Beyond Borders — Giving Back, Investing, and Expanding Your Impact

When you first land in a new country, your dream is simple: Survive. Make it. Send something home.

But as time passes, the definition of success begins to change. It's no longer just about you — it's about the *footprints* you'll leave behind.

Every successful immigrant eventually asks:

"What will my story mean when I'm gone?"

That's where legacy begins.

1. What Legacy Really Means

Legacy isn't about how much money you make.
It's about *who you became while making it,* and *who you helped along the way.*

Legacy is the scholarship fund you start in your village.
It's the nephew who looks at you and says,

"If Uncle Shola could do it, so can I."

It's your kids watching your consistency and learning that *greatness is built, not given.*

Your true wealth isn't in your bank, it's in your impact.

2. The Man Who Never Forgot His Roots

Fidelis left Nigeria with $200 in his pocket.
He worked factory shifts, studied at night, and eventually became a nurse.

When his life stabilized, he didn't just focus on himself, he started a small foundation back home.
He began sponsoring two kids through school each year.

Ten years later, those two kids became eight.
One of them, Esther, later graduated as a nurse, just like him.

He said,

"I couldn't save everyone, but I could change someone's story."

That's the ripple effect of a purposeful life.

3. The Two Types of Legacy

There are two sides to legacy:

1. Generational Legacy (Family)

- Teaching your children financial discipline, respect, and vision.
- Building assets — not just cash — that can sustain them.
- Leaving behind wisdom, not just wealth.

2. Social Legacy (Community)

- Mentoring younger immigrants.
- Supporting causes that align with your values.
- Building businesses that employ others.
- Giving back to your home country or community abroad.

A true blueprint of success balances both.

4. The Power of Planting Back Home

Many immigrants struggle with whether to invest back home, scared of corruption or loss.

And yes, you must be cautious — but *never disconnected.*

You can build wisely by:

- Partnering with trusted relatives or professionals.
- Starting small (land, property, or micro-business).
- Verifying everything legally.
- Treating it like a real investment, not a favor.

You left home for opportunity, not abandonment.
Building back home doesn't weaken your growth; it *anchors* it.

5. The Woman Who Built a School from Her Savings

Ruth from Kenya worked as a caregiver in the U.S. for years. Every month, she sent a small part of her income to build a classroom back home.

What started as one classroom grew into a small primary school with over 80 children.
Now, she visits every year to oversee it.

She said,

"I didn't build a mansion. I built minds."

That's what legacy looks like: something that continues when you're not there.

6. Investing the Smart Way

Once you're stable financially, start thinking about how to make your money *work for you*.

Here's a simple roadmap:

1. **Emergency Fund** — 3–6 months of expenses.
2. **Debt Reduction** — Pay off high-interest debt.
3. **Retirement Accounts** — 401(k), IRA, or Roth IRA.
4. **Investments** — Stocks, ETFs, real estate, or business ventures.
5. **Insurance** — Protect your life, health, and assets.
6. **Estate Planning** — Write a will. Don't leave your family confused.

Financial wisdom isn't just survival — it's *freedom*.

7. The Couple Who Built Quiet Wealth

Juliet and Emmanuel, a Haitian couple, worked regular jobs, nothing fancy.
They saved aggressively, invested in a duplex, and rented out one side.

After five years, they refinanced and bought another property. Now, their rentals pay their mortgage, and their children will inherit assets, not debts.

They said,

"We didn't chase status. We built stability."

That's the difference between looking rich and *being wealthy.*

8. Mentorship: Lifting Others As You Rise

Every immigrant who makes it has a duty: **teach someone behind you.**

Mentorship isn't about money, it's about guidance.
It's the advice you wish someone gave you when you first landed.

You can mentor a younger student, a new arrival, or even a relative back home.

Because one conversation can save someone *years* of confusion.

9. Story: The Mechanic Who Became a Mentor

Carlos, a Mexican immigrant in Texas, started as a mechanic's apprentice.
He later opened his own auto shop.

Instead of hoarding knowledge, he began training young immigrants, teaching them how to fix cars, speak with customers, and build confidence.

Now, five of his former trainees run their own garages.

He said,

"My real business isn't fixing cars. It's fixing lives."

10. Balancing Two Worlds

Being an immigrant means living between two homes — your new world and your old one.
It's easy to feel torn between them.

But balance is possible.

- Build your foundation in the U.S.
- Stay emotionally connected to your roots.
- Let your success bridge both worlds.

You are not *from one place anymore.*
You are the link between two nations.

11. Story: Dual Citizenship, Dual Purpose

Bisi from Nigeria became a U.S. citizen but never stopped identifying with home.
She invests in local farming cooperatives in Nigeria while running a small tech company in Atlanta.

She said,

"I don't have to choose between the two worlds. I build in both."

That's the beauty of the immigrant spirit — *adaptation without erasure.*

12. The Final Stage: Purpose Over Possession

At some point, success stops being about money.
It becomes about *meaning.*

You start realizing it's not what you own, but what you *inspire.*

Purposeful living means:

- You work hard, but not endlessly.
- You give, but wisely.
- You chase dreams, but not at the cost of peace.

Because peace — real peace — is the true definition of success.

13. The Taxi Driver Who Became a Donor

Ahmed, a Somali taxi driver in Minnesota, was known for working long hours.

Quietly, he began donating $100 a month to build wells in villages back home.

Years later, he visited one of the sites and saw children drinking clean water.

He broke down crying.

He said,

"I thought I was just sending money. But I was sending hope."

14. Legacy Isn't About the End — It's About Continuity

Legacy is not a destination — it's a relay.
You pass the baton to those who come after you.

You've fought too hard for your story to die with you.
Let it multiply — through others, through your work, through your impact.

15. Closing Message: You Are the Blueprint

You are not just another immigrant — you are a living **blueprint.**

Someone somewhere is studying your courage.
Someone is being inspired by your silence, your grind, your grace.

You may not realize it, but your story is already teaching others how to believe.

So keep building.
Keep saving.
Keep growing.
Keep giving.

And when the world asks how you did it, tell them proudly:

"I followed the Successful Immigrant Blueprint — I built my dream with discipline, focus, and faith."

Final Quote to Close the Book:

"You came as a dreamer. You stayed as a doer. You'll be remembered as a builder."

Conclusion:

The Blueprint Was You All Along

When you left your home country, you didn't just cross an ocean,
you crossed into a new version of yourself.

Maybe you came with fear. Maybe you came with hope.
Maybe you came with nothing but a dream and a bag full of faith.

But through every struggle, every lonely night, every silent prayer, you kept moving.
You adjusted your tongue to a new accent.
You stretched your dollars.
You smiled through exhaustion.
And even when the world didn't see you, *you kept building anyway.*

That's what makes you extraordinary.

The truth is, this book was never just about saving money, studying, or starting a business.
It was about **becoming.**

Becoming focused.
Becoming fearless.
Becoming free.

You see, the *Successful Immigrant Blueprint* isn't written on paper — it's written in your journey.

Every sacrifice, every rejection, every tiny win was a *page* in your own story.

You've proven that success isn't about luck or location — it's about *discipline, clarity, and faith.*

You didn't come here to survive.
You came here to *build.*

Build peace.
Build confidence.
Build wealth.
Build legacy.

And when you build, you give others permission to dream again.

To the Dreamer Reading This

If you're reading this right now — exhausted, confused, or uncertain — let this be your reminder:
You are not behind. You are *becoming.*

Don't compare your chapter two to someone else's chapter ten. Your time is coming — and when it does, you'll realize every delay was preparing you.

Keep showing up.
Keep learning.
Keep saving.
Keep praying.

Because one day, someone will look at you and say,

"Because of you, I didn't give up."

That's the moment you'll know you didn't just make it — you made *meaning*.

Author's Note: From Shola to You

When I first thought about writing this book, I didn't want to write another "how to make it" manual.
I wanted to write a mirror, something that shows what it *really* means to be an immigrant with fire in your heart and purpose in your steps.

I've met people who started with nothing but faith and now they're business owners, homeowners, and mentors.
I've seen how courage can turn a janitor into a CEO, and how humility can build bridges between continents.

I've also seen the loneliness, the confusion, the pressure to "make it" fast and I know how heavy that can feel.

So, if you take one thing from this book, let it be this:

You already have what it takes.
You are the blueprint.

This book isn't the end, it's the beginning.
My hope is that you use it as a foundation and then build your own story boldly, fearlessly, and unapologetically.

And when you do, when your business grows, when your family thrives, when your story becomes a testimony,
I want you to reach back, and lift someone else up.

That's the circle of success.
That's how legacies are born.
That's how immigrants become icons.

Final Words:

This is your time.
Your story matters.
Your vision is valid.
And your dream — no matter how far away it seems — is possible.

You came to this land as a dreamer.
Now Walk through it as a *builder*.

Because the blueprint is in your hands.
And the world is waiting for what only you can create.

Quote to End the Book:

"The immigrant's journey is not about finding a place to belong, it's about creating one."

SHOLA OYEWOLE

The 90-Day Action Plan: Turning Your Blueprint Into Results

Congratulations, you've made it through the *Successful Immigrant Blueprint.*
But your real journey starts now.

Reading the book was the *first step.*
Now it's time to *build your own blueprint.*

Over the next 90 days, you'll create focus, discipline, and momentum — one habit, one action, one decision at a time.

You don't need to do everything at once.
You just need to *start.*

Let's break it down.

Phase 1: Foundation (Days 1–30)

"Stability Before Expansion"

This first month is about **control** over your money, your mind, and your environment.

Step 1: Financial Reset

Goal: Know where your money is going.

Action Points:

- Track every expense for 30 days (use an app or notebook).
- Identify your top 3 money leaks (e.g., food delivery, subscriptions, impulsive spending).

- Open a separate **savings account** — name it *Freedom Fund*.
- Set a small weekly savings target (even $20 counts).

Reflection Prompt:

What habit is costing me the most, and what can I do differently starting this week?

Step 2: Language and Learning Growth

Goal: Polish your communication and knowledge.

Action Points:

- Spend 20 minutes daily reading, listening, or speaking in English.
- Watch one educational video per week on your career or business topic.
- Join one free online class, local library group, or workshop.

Reflection Prompt:

What's one area of learning that can unlock my next level of opportunity?

Step 3: Environment Check

Goal: Surround yourself with progress.

Action Points:

- Clean and organize your living space — order creates clarity.

- Limit time with people who drain your energy.
- Write down the names of 3 people who motivate you — spend more time learning from them.

Reflection Prompt:

Who do I need to spend less time with and who do I need to learn from more?

Phase 2: Growth (Days 31–60)

"Action Over Intention"

This phase is about building systems, not just dreams.

Step 1: Career or Business Building

Goal: Move from thinking to doing.

Action Points:

- Create a short-term business or career goal (e.g., register my business, apply for a certification, start a side hustle).
- Do one action weekly toward it.
- Tell one trusted person your goal — accountability builds momentum.

Reflection Prompt:

What fear has stopped me from taking this step before and how can I face it now?

Step 2: Visibility and Confidence

Goal: Stop hiding. Share your skills.

Action Points:

- Update your LinkedIn, résumé, or online profile.
- Share one thing you're working on — no bragging, just courage.
- Practice introducing yourself with pride (your accent is part of your story, not your flaw).

Reflection Prompt:

What am I good at that I've been afraid to showcase and why?

Step 3: Ghost Mode Discipline

Goal: Build quietly. Deliver loudly.

Action Points:

- Choose one goal and work in silence for 30 days.
- Wake up one hour earlier, use that hour for your project or reading.
- Reduce social media scrolling by 50%.

Reflection Prompt:

What would my life look like if I stayed consistent for just 30 days straight?

Phase 3: Legacy (Days 61–90)

"Multiply Your Impact"

Now it's time to think *beyond yourself.*

Step 1: Community and Giving Back

Goal: Share your progress — even in small ways.

Action Points:

- Mentor one person, even informally.
- Support a cause that connects with your story.
- Celebrate your 60-day progress — you've earned it.

Reflection Prompt:

Who can I help this month, using the lessons I've already learned?

Step 2: Build Assets, Not Just Income

Goal: Begin planting seeds for your future.

Action Points:

- Research simple investments (ETFs, savings accounts, or side businesses).
- Set a long-term goal: "In 2 years, I want to own _____."
- Read or watch one video weekly about financial literacy.

Reflection Prompt:

If I could build one source of wealth in the next 2 years, what would it be?

Step 3: Celebrate Your Growth

Goal: Reflect, refine, and reimagine.

Action Points:

- Write a letter to yourself — thanking you for not giving up.
- Write down 3 things you've achieved since Day 1.
- Create a new 90-day plan — because growth never ends.

Reflection Prompt:

What have I learned about myself that I didn't know before?

The 90-Day Commitment Declaration

Read this out loud and sign it:

"I commit to showing up for myself for the next 90 days, with focus, faith, and consistency.
I will honor my dreams by working for them daily.
I will not compare my pace to anyone else's.
I will think, act, and save like the builder I am becoming.
I am the blueprint.
And I will succeed."

Signature: _____
Date: _____

Final Encouragement from Shola:

You don't have to move fast, you just have to move forward. One step at a time. One day at a time.

And by the end of these 90 days, you'll look back and realize: You didn't just follow the *Successful Immigrant Blueprint.* You *became it.*

www.ingramcontent.com/pod-product-compliance
Lightning Source LLC
Chambersburg PA
CBHW071227090426
42736CB00014B/2994